THIS DICTIONARY
and every word in it,
from A to Z,
BELONGS TO:

_____

quiet
buzz
wagon
yellow
pirate
table
refrigerator
rat
cow
ouch
vacation
lion
tongue
kitchen
umbrella
sea
up
kite
ostrich
juice
whack
gasoline
lion
early
yet
yell
breakfast
owl
newspaper
firefly
hop
ivy
accident
X-ray
zyxuzpf
junkyard
jelly sandwich
lasso
jet
ice cream
quart
moon
mustard
cheese
alphabet
kite
raincoat
xanthophyll
Indian
ivy
wag
yard
X-ray
valentine
junkyard
Halloween
noodle
freeze
ax
shadow
Oobooglunk
key
yawn
tricycle
joke
magic
nine
hard
television
ice skates
hop
rabbit
vaccination
wait
whale
balloon
knife
net

The Cat in the Hat

Beginner Book

DICTIONARY

by the Cat himself
and
P.D. Eastman

BEGINNER BOOKS

A Division of Random House, Inc.

This dictionary has a serious purpose.

There is nothing more serious than helping a child learn how to read.

But the Editors of Beginner Books, who put this dictionary together, decided they could be serious…and still avoid being stuffy.

So they made this book of words just as funny as they could make it.

It's full of ridiculous alligators, foolish bears and giraffes' uncles, all racing around and getting involved in nonsensical adventures.

The average child, we've discovered, seems to like things just that way. And that is fine. It helps us to focus the child's attention on the serious job we're trying to accomplish…to make him recognize, remember, *and really enjoy* a basic elementary vocabulary of 1350 words.

*   *   *

We offer you no rules on how to use this book with your children.

Maybe, the first time around, you'll want to read it to them.

The second time around, they may read some of it to *you*.

Dr. Seuss

A a

Aaron

Aaron is an alligator.

about

Aaron is about to go up.

above

Aaron above the clouds

accident

Accident. Poor Aaron!

across

Abigail going across

add

Abigail is adding.

afraid

Abigail is afraid.

after

A mouse after a cat

again

Aaron is up again.

ah

Say "ah."

ahead

The cat is ahead of the mouse.

3

airplane

Airplanes

along

"Come along."

alike

All alike

alphabet

alone

All alone

always

Aaron is
always having accidents.

4

American

American Indian

ant

Ants in pants

angry

An **angry** animal

any

Are there **any** more ants
anywhere around?

another

Another angry animal

apple

Arms full of **apples**

answer

Answer it! **Answer** it!

arrow

aunt

Abigail's Aunt Ada

ask

Abigail asking for an apple

auto

Aunt Ada's auto

asleep

Aaron asleep

Aaron awake

away

Away goes Aunt Ada.

ax

6

B b

baby

bad

back

A baby on an animal's back   7   **A bad baby**

bag
baggage

balloon

Baby likes balloons.

bake

A baker baking bread

banana

Baby likes bananas.

band

ball

Baseball   **Football**

bank

A piggy bank

barber

Aaron at the barber's

bark

Dogs do it.

barn

basket

A baby in a basket

bat

Aunt Ada batting

bath

Bathtub   Shower bath

9

bear

bell

Ringing bells

bed

A bear in bed in his bedroom

belt

A bear with a belt

bee

Bees after a bear

beside

A bear beside a tree

behind

A bear behind a tree

between

A bear between trees

bicycle

Aunt Ada's bike

big

Big   Bigger   Biggest

bird

birthday

A bird's birthday cake

bit

He bit a big bite.

black

A blackbird at a blackboard

block

blow

A breeze is blowing.

blue

body

Bones in a body

book

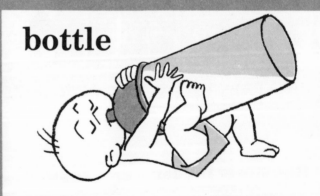

A book about birds

boot

Bird boots

bottle

bowl

Bananas in a bowl

box

Bananas in a **box**

breathe

Breathe in. **Breathe** out.

boy

Boy bear   **Girl** bear

brick

Bricks

break

Breaking the bank

breakfast

Breakfast in bed

bridge

A baby in a boat in a brook
under a **bridge**

13

bright

Bright light

bring

"Bring me a balloon, boy."

broom

brother

A bear and his brother

brush

A bear brushing

bubble

Bubble gum

build

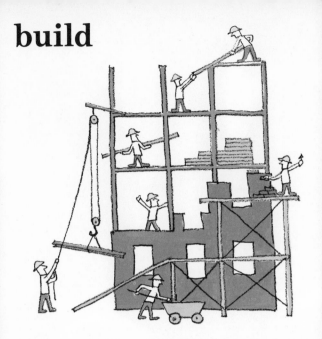

Builders building **a** building

bus

butter

A butterfly **on the** butter

bump

button

Big blue buttons

burn

I burned it.

buzz

Bees buzz by.

C c

cactus

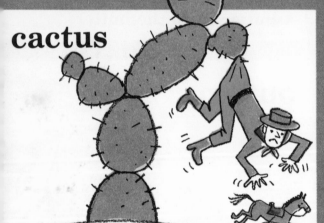

Cowboy caught on a cactus

cage

An animal in a cage

calf

A cow's child

call

"HERE, CAMEL, CAMEL, CAMEL."

Aunt Ada calling her camel

16

camera

camp

Campfire

can

"I can't open this can! Can you?"

candle

candy

Chocolate candy

cap

We all have caps.

car

Car   Cart

17

castle

cent

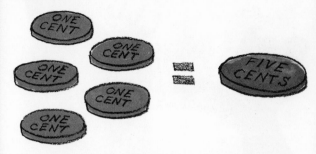

Five cents make a nickel.

chair

Bears in chairs

catch

Catching the ball

chase

Chasing a fly

ceiling

A fly on the ceiling

cheese

"I love it."

18

chicken

Chicken   Chicks

child

Child   Children

chimney

Santa Claus comes down it.

chin

Christmas

Merry Christmas

church

circle

All in a circle

city

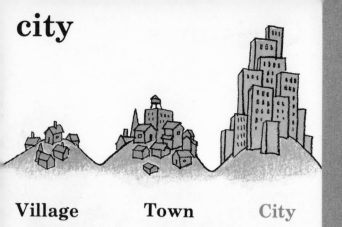

Village   Town   City

clean

Cleaning the city

climb

Climbers climbing

clock

Alarm clock   Cuckoo clock

clothes

Clothes   Clothesline   Clothespins

clown

Circus clown

coat

20

Aunt Ada's fur coat

cold

come

"Come!"   He came.

colors

cook

A cook cooking a cookie

comb

corn

Corn   Popcorn

21

corner

A mouse in a corner

cow

Cow   Calf   Bull

could

He could.   He couldn't.

crack

A crack in the mirror

count

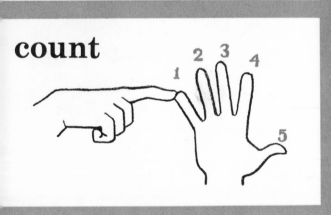

crash

Aaron crashed again.

country

City

Country

crayon

Baby likes crayons.

crow

cry

Babies do it.

crowd

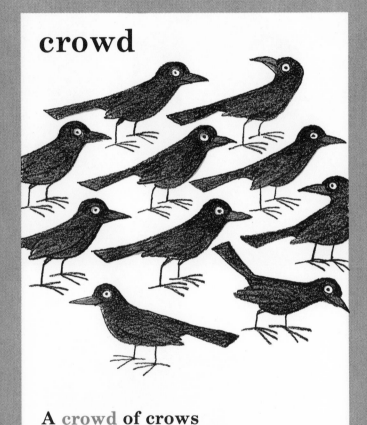

A crowd of crows

cup

Cup and saucer

crown

cut

Aaron cutting

Dd

dad

"My **daddy** is dancing with Aaron."

dark

deep

Dark night   **Light** day   24   **Down** deep

dentist

Aaron at the dentist's

dinner

Cooking dinner

dinosaur

dishes

Dirty dishes

dive

Aunt Ada diving

do

The "do" words

did

does

doesn't

doing

don't

done

doctor

Dog doctor

25

doll

A dollar doll

down

up

down

door

"Close that door."

dozen

A dozen doughnuts   Twelve

draw

Drawing **a duck**

dot

Dots

dream

Dreaming **about dresses**

drink

A deer drinking

drip

Drops are dripping.

drum

dry

Drying her hair

dump

dust

E e

ear

early

An early bird

east

Big ears

28

A bird going east

eat

Eating eight eggs

eleven

He ate eleven.

electric

Electric shaver

empty

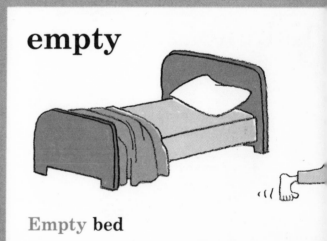

Empty **bed**

elephant

end

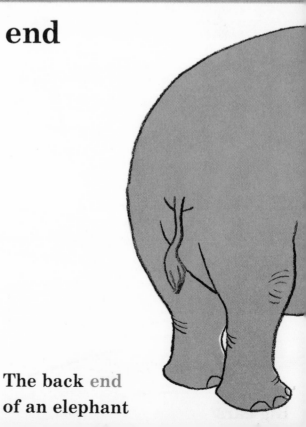

The back end of an elephant

29

entrance

exercise

Aunt Ada exercising

Eskimo

explode

eye

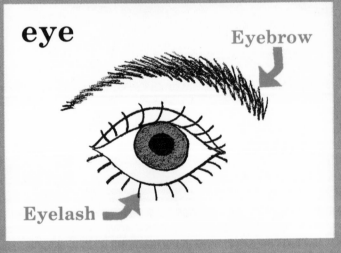

Eyebrow

Eyelash

every

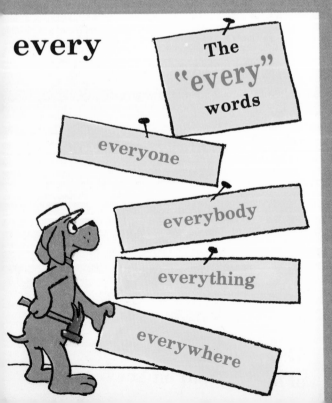

The "every" words

everyone

everybody

everything

everywhere

eyeglasses

F f

fairy

face

fall

"Wash your face."

31

The fairy fell on her face.

family

A large family

farm

A farmer farming on a farm

fan

Electric fan

fast

Fast   **Faster**   **Fastest**

far

The star is far away.

fat

A fat bear   **A thin bear**

father

"That is my father."

feather

Fine feathers

feed

Feeding spinach to the baby

feel

Father feels awful.

feet

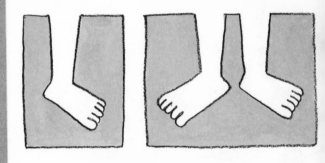

Foot   Feet

fence

Feet on a fence

33

few

A few fish

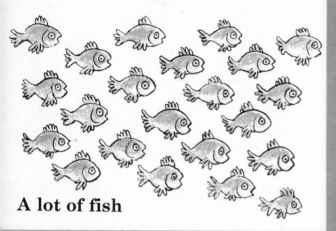

A lot of fish

fight

fill

"Fill it full."

find

Finding a nickel

finger

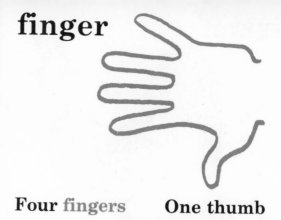

Four fingers   One thumb

fire

Firemen on a fire engine
going to a fire

firefly

first

First   **Second** **Third**

five

Five pelicans

fix

"Can you fix it, Father?"

flag

Flags on a boat

flashlight

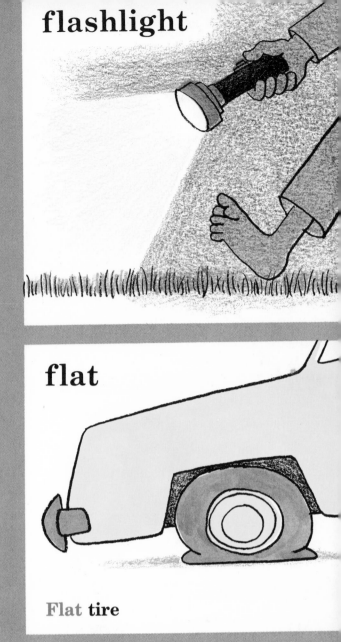

flat

Flat tire

float

Father floating

35

floor

Ceiling

Floor

follow

Follow the leader.

flower

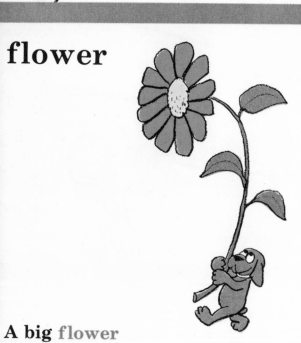

A big flower

food

fly

Aaron is flying again.

36

fork

Knife   Fork

found

He **found** a fox in the forest.

freeze

"IT'S FREEZING IN HERE."

Food freezer

four

Four foxes

fresh

A **fresh egg**

free

friend

37

Friendly frogs

frown

Frowning

fruit

grapes

pear

grapefruit

pineapple

watermelon

lemon

banana

fun

G g

game

A **game** of cards

garbage

Aunt Ada's garbage

garage

Aunt Ada's garage

garden

Flower garden

39

gargle

A gargling bear

get

"What did you get for Christmas? We got a bike."

gasoline

"Give me a gallon."

gave

He gave him a gallon.

giant

A great big man

giraffe

glove

Boxing gloves

go

The sun goes down.
The sun is going down.

glad

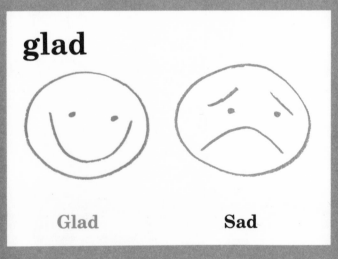

Glad   Sad

gone

The sun is gone.

glass

good

Good dog   Bad dog

41

good-by

grandfather

My father   **My grandfather**

goose

Goose   Geese

grape

Sour grapes

grass

Goats eat grass.

grade

First grade   Second grade

42

grasshopper

Grasshoppers **hopping**

gray

grow

"My flowers have grown."

groceries

guess

"Guess who!"

ground

Under the ground

43

gun

Popgun

H h

hair

"I have three of them."

hall

half

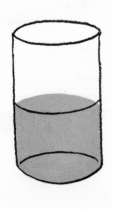

Halloween

Half **full**

44

ham

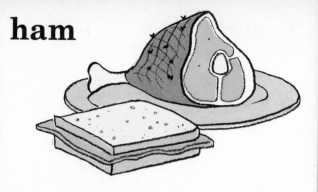

Ham **sandwich**

hammer

Hammering

hand

Shaking hands

hang

"Hang **it on the** hanger."

happen

"Everything happens **to me.**"

happy

"Happy **birthday to us!**"

hard

Hard **bed**

Soft bed

45

hat

His hat **Her hat**

heart

Heart   Club   Diamond   Spade

hay

Cows eat it.

heavy

head

Aunt Ada on her head

helicopter

Aunt Ada's helicopter

hear

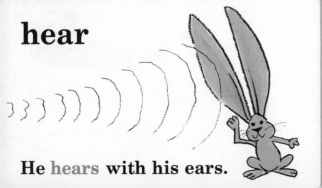

He hears with his ears.

hello

hide

Aaron is hiding.

help

high

Up high

Down low

hen

"My mother is a hen."

hit

Clown hitting clown

here

Hair here   No hair there

47

hold

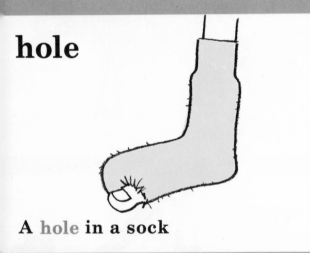

Holding the baby

hole

Christmas is a holiday.

A hole in a sock

holiday

Christmas is a holiday.

hollow

Hollow tree

home

"This is my home."

honey

PURE
HONEY

Bees make it.

honk

Geese do it.

horse

hook

Fishhook

hot

A hot horse

hop

Frogs do it.

hour

Hour hand

Minute hand

horn

A goat with three horns

49

house

A horse in a house

hump

One hump

Two humps

hungry

They are hungry.

hunt

Hunting ducks

hurry

"Don't hurry so."

hurt

50

He hurried and he got hurt.

I i

ice cream

ice skates

igloo

An Eskimo house

inch

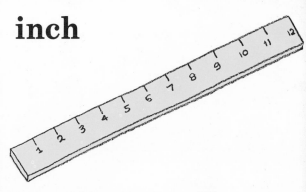

51

Twelve inches   A foot

Indian

An American
Indian

An Indian from India

iron

An Indian ironing his pants
on an island

ink

itch

"I itch."

insect

"I have insects
inside my igloo."

ivy

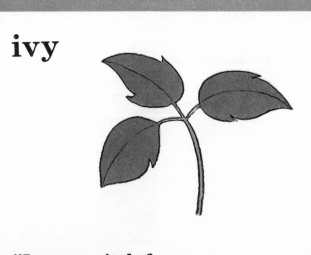

"I got my itch from
poison ivy."

Jack

James

Jerry

Joe

jacket

Jack in a jacket

jam

James at the jam jar

jack-o-lantern

Jack's jack-o-lantern

jelly

Jerry in the jelly jar

jet

Jerry in his jet

joke

Joe playing a joke on Jack

juice

Jack likes juice.

jump

James jumps over Jack and Joe.

jungle

Jerry in a jungle

junk

Jack, James, Jerry, and Joe in a junk yard

K k

kangaroo

kerchoo

Sneezers do it.

keep

key

Keyhole

"Keep **away** from the kangaroo."

55

kick

Aunt Ada is a good kicker.

king

kill

Kill that fly.

kiss

Kissed by a king

kind

Two kinds of birds

kite

"Don't fly kites in the kitchen."

56

kitten

A cat's child

knees

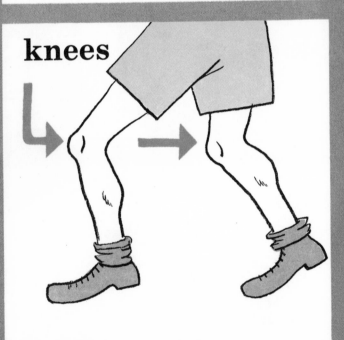

knife

"Don't eat with your knife."

knock

Knocking

know

"I know he is going to fall down."

"I knew it."

57

L l

ladder

A lady on a ladder

lamb

"My child is a lamb."

lake

Lake Minnihaweetonka

land

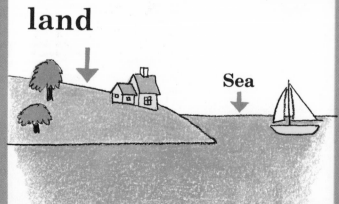

Sea

58

lap

Sitting on laps

late

Late for school

lasso

laugh

Laughing   **Crying**

last

The last pretzel

lazy

"We all feel lazy."

learn

"He is learning to fly."

leg

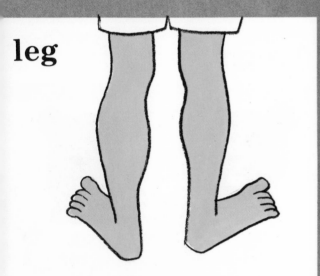

Left leg   **Right leg**

let

"Let me out of here."

letter

Letter box

library

Books!   **Books!**   **Books!**

lick

lie

"Lie down."

He lay down.

lift

Aaron lifting a lot of lemons

light

The lighthouse light is lit.

lightning

lion

Aunt Ada likes lions.

lip

Lips

listen

Listening

lollipops

Baby likes them.

little

Little bird   Big bird

long

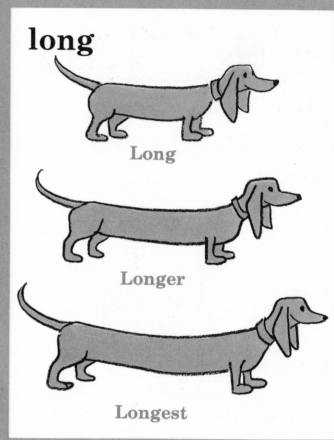

Long

Longer

Longest

log

A frog on a log

look

Looking for a lost sock

62

loose

The goose is loose.

luck

Lucky four leaf clover

loud

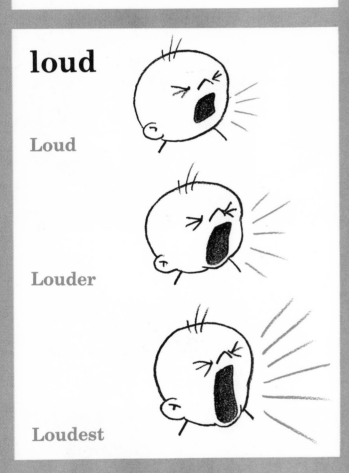

Loud

Louder

Loudest

lump

One lump

love

She loves her baby.

lunch

Lunch box

M m

machine

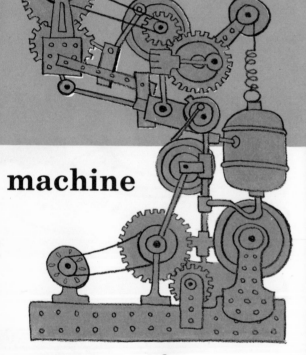

Machinery

made

"I made it all by myself."

magic

A magician doing magic

mail

Mailbag **Mailman** **Mailbox**

map

A **map** of the United States

make

Aaron is **making** more machines.

marble

A game of **marbles**

man

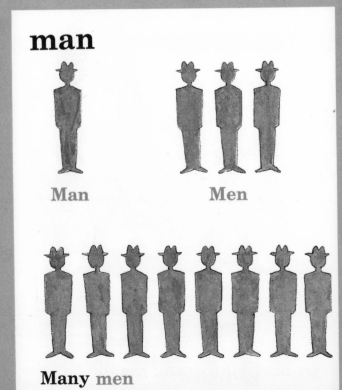

Man **Men**

Many **men**

mask

A moose **mask**

65

mat

Door mat

match

Be careful.
Little matches make big fires.

may
maybe

He may dive in.
Maybe he will.
He might.   He might not.

meat
meet

Meeting at the meat market

meow

Cats do it.

merry

66

Merry-go-round

mess

An awful **mess**

minute

Five **minutes** to five

midnight

Midnight is the middle of the night.

miss

He **missed** the bus.

million

There are **millions** of stars.

mitten

"We all have **mittens**."

mix

The cook is mixing eggs and flour.

money

Jack has more money than Joe.

monkey

A monkey with a monkey wrench

month

The twelve months

moo

Cows do it.

They also give milk.

68

moon

Aaron is going there.

morning

"What a beautiful morning!"

mother

"She is the mother of me."

mountain

Mountain   Hill

mouth

Open mouth   Shut mouth

69

move

Moving to another house

movie

Mr. and Mrs.

Mr. Mouse   Mrs. Mouse

mud

Aunt Ada is stuck in the mud.

music

Making music

must
mustard

"You must not eat
so much mustard."

N n

nail

name

"My name is Tom."

"My name is Oobooglunk."

near

Oobooglunk lives near Nubbglubb.

71

neck

Necktie

never

"He will never get me."

need

"We need a bath."

new

New shoe   Old shoe

nest

newspaper

THE DAILY NEWS

net

next

"I am next."

night

nine

Nine nights

no

No more left
None
Not a drop

noise

"Stop that noise."

noodle

Noodle soup

noon

The middle of the day

north

A bird flying north

73

nose

Little nose   **Big** nose

nurse

Aaron's nurse

nothing

Nothing **at all**

now

"It is now **four-thirty."**

nut

Coconut

numbers

39,570,868

33 $\frac{1}{3}$

100

428

2

65

$\frac{1}{7}$

12

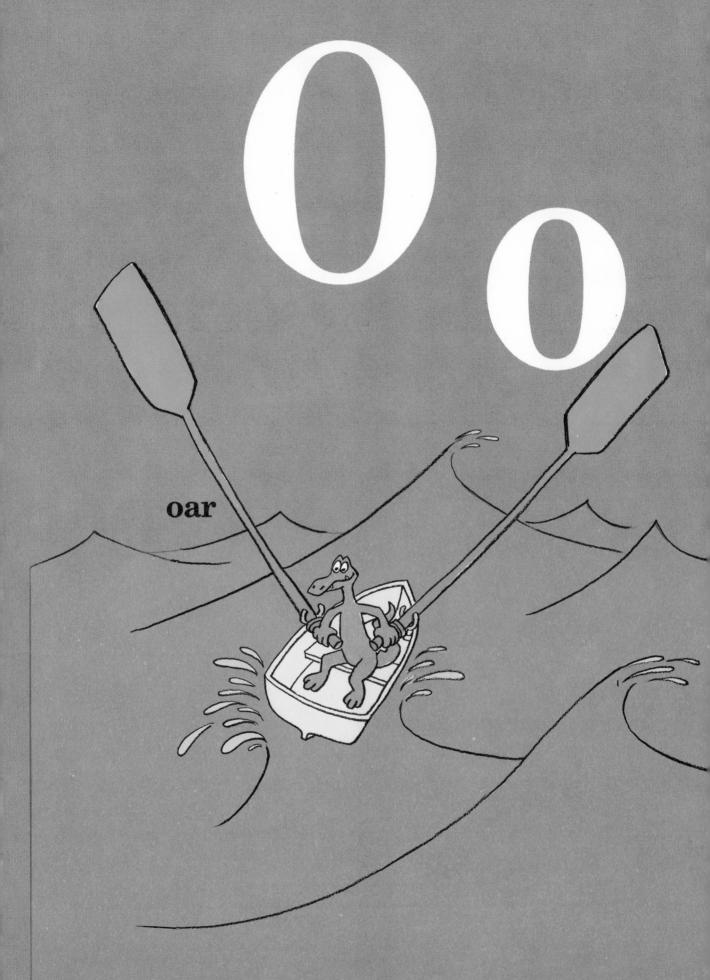

O o

oar

ocean

off

"Oh! I fell off."

office

Father's office

often

"I fall off often."

oil

Oiling the bike

old

An old, old mouse

one

One onion   Only one

open

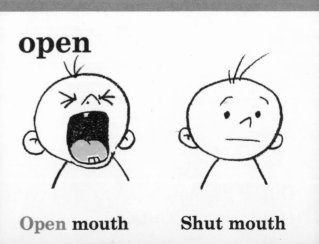

Open mouth   Shut mouth

ostrich

"Our own ostrich"

over

Over a cloth

other

One orange is green.
The other orange is orange.

overalls

Overalls on Aaron

ouch

out

Out of the house
Outdoors   Outside

owl

"We own our own owl."

P p

pack

Packing **his suitcase**

paddle

Canoe **paddle**

package

Carrying packages

page

Books have pages.

pails

palace

"My house"

paint

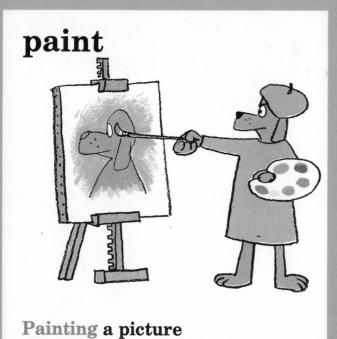

Painting a picture

pan

A pan full of pancakes

pants

A pair of pants

pajamas

Aaron likes pretty pajamas.

papa

Another name for dear old daddy

79

paper

The paper boy

parachute

parade

A parade in a park

part

A centaur is part man and part horse.

party

Birthday party

past

Half past nine

pat

Patting the dog

paw

A dog's hand

pay

Paying for the tickets

peanuts

Peanut shells

pedal

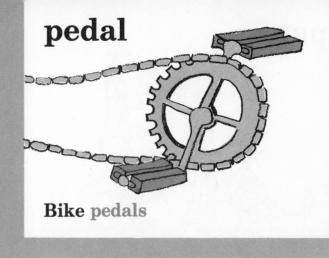

Bike pedals

pen
pencil

**A penguin
with a pen and a pencil**

people

People　　　　　**Animals**

pepper

Pepper　　　　　**Salt**

pet

Cats and dogs are good pets.

piano

pick

Picking up after the picnic

phone

Phoning from a phone booth

pie

A piece of pumpkin pie

phonograph

pig

A pink pig on a pillow

pin

Safety pin

plant

**Planting
a jum-jum plant**

pinch

Crabs do it.

plate

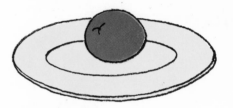

A plum on a plate

pirate

play

pitcher

**A pitcher full of
jum-jum juice**

83

Playing on the playground

please

PLEASE KEEP OFF THE GRASS

pockets

Kangaroos have them.

point

Pointing

pole

Pole vaulting

police

"I am a police horse."

pony

Pony   Pony cart

pool

Swimming pool

pop

"My pop is popping popcorn."

porpoise

Happy porpoises

pot

Hot pot

potato

Hot potato

pound

A sixteen-pound baby

pour

Pouring the jum-jum juice

prize

push

Aunt Ada pushing her car

puddle

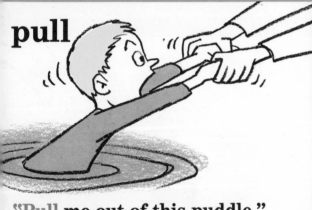

put

Putting out the cat

pull

"Pull me out of this puddle."

pup
puppy

"This pup is my puppy."

puzzle

Puzzled by a puzzle

Qq

quack

Ducks do it.

quart

A quart of milk

quick

"Quick," said the queen.
"Take this milk away quickly."

queen

A quart of milk
for the queen

quiet

The quiet milkman took
the quart away quietly.

question

The queen asked a question:
"Is this milk fresh?"
"No, queen. It is old milk,"
answered the milkman.

R r

rabbit

race

A rabbit race
The rabbits are racing.

radio

Hearing news on the radio

rain

Rain is raining
on the rabbits.

raincoat

Rabbits racing in raincoats

ranch

"I am a cowboy.
I live on a ranch."

rat

read

A rat reading

red

refrigerator

reindeer

"There is a reindeer
in our refrigerator."

remember

"I know that bear, but
I can't remember his name."

rest

A long man having
a long rest

ribbon

Hair ribbons

rich

The king is rich.

ride

"We are riding a rhinoceros."

right

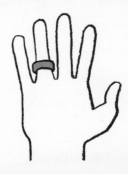

Left foot   Right foot

ring

91

ring

Our phone rang.
It is always ringing.

rock

Rocky mountains

river

Ducks on a river

rocket

A rocket
over rocky mountains

road

Ducks on a road

rode
rodeo

The cowboy
rode at the rodeo.

roll

Aunt Ada rolling on roller skates

rooster

A hen's husband

roof

Roller skating on the roof

rope

room

"My room is a mess."

rose

A bunch of roses for the queen

round

Hoops are round.

row

Rowing in a rowboat

row

Five robins in a row

rub

Cats like to rub on chairs.

rug

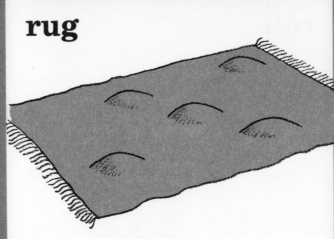

Five robins under a rug

run

The running rhinoceros ran to Rochester.

S s

sad

A sad, sad dog

saddle

safe

"He can't get me. I'm safe."

95

sail

A **sailor** **sailing**
in a **sailboat**

sandwich

A big **sandwich**

same

"We look alike.
We look the **same**."

sank

"My sailboat **sank**."

sand

Sandbox

save

People **save** money.

Squirrels **save** nuts.

saw

"I see a saw."

saw

"I saw a seesaw."

say

Baby said something.
But what did he say?

scissors

scooter

scratch

Dogs do it.

sea
seal

A seal in the sea

season

There are four seasons.

Spring

Autumn

Summer

Winter

seeds

Plant them.

They grow.

sell

"He sells hot dogs.
He sold one to me."

send
sent

Mother sent us to bed.

set

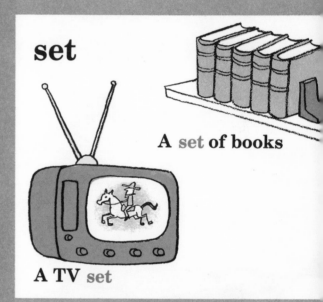

A set of books

A TV set

seven

Seven sisters

99

sew

Seven sisters sewing shirts

sharp

Needles are sharp.

shadow

Aunt Ada's shadow

she

"I am a boy bird.
She is a girl bird."

shake

Shaking paws

sheep

100

shell

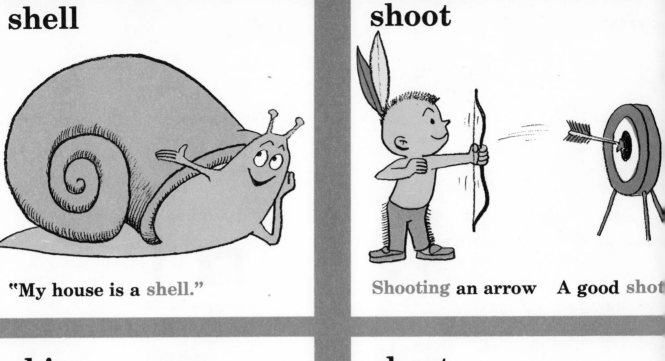

"My house is a shell."

shoot

Shooting an arrow   A good shot

shine

Shoeshine

short

"My shirt is too short."

ship

A big boat

shout

CAN YOU HEAR ME

Shouting

show

Daddy **showed** his movies.
It was not a good **show**.

side

Left side   **Right** side

Inside   Outside

shut
shutters

Shutting the shutters

sign

EAT Helen's FUDGE

COS COB

DRINK ZOX

WACO

MOTEL

AZUSA

Signboards

sick

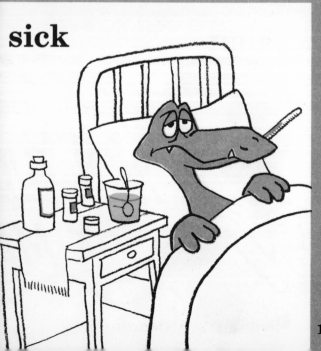

silly

Making a silly face

102

sing

Seven sisters
singing songs

sit

The seven sisters sat down.
They are sitting on a seat.

six

Six skunks

skate

A skunk on skates

sky

"We fly in the sky."

sled

sleep

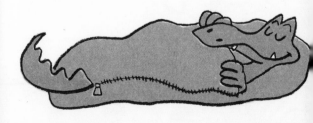

Sleeping in a sleeping bag

slide

Sliding

smell

Skunks do.

slow

Slow   Fast

smile

small

Small Smaller Smallest

smoke

Smoking **chimneys**

snack

Eating a snack in a shack

sneeze

A snake sneezing

sniff

snort

Bulls do it.

snow

Snowflakes

Snowman

Snowball

Snowshoes

Snowshovel

soap

Soapsuds

sock

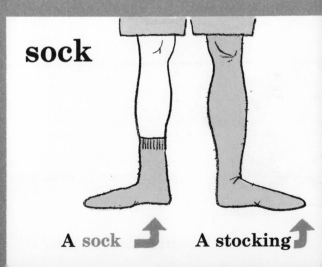

A sock   A stocking

105

some

somebody

somehow

someone

something

sometimes

somewhere

The "some" words

spider

Spider web

south

W N S E

A bird going south

spill

Spilled milk

spell

"How do you spell Llewellyn?"

spin

A spinning top

splash

Elephants make big ones.

spot

"They call me Spot."

stair

Going down the stairs

stamp

You lick it. You stick it.

stand

Soldiers standing at attention

start

Aunt Ada can't start her car.

station

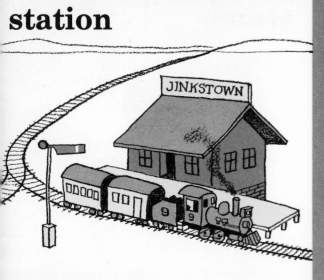

Railroad station

stick

Smart dogs fetch sticks.

stay

"You stay home.
You can't come along."

still

Standing still

steps

Steep steps

sting

Mosquitoes do it.

stone

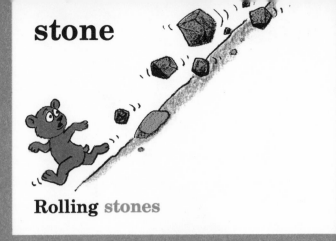

Rolling stones

street

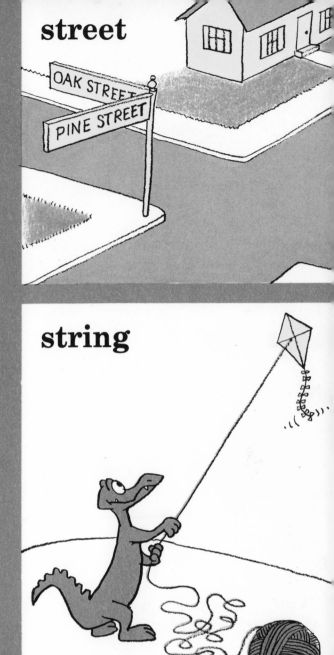

stop

Aaron stopped.

string

Kite string

story

A bedtime story

straight

suit

Straight hair **Curly hair** 109 **Suits in a store**

sun

On Sunday it was sunny.
Daddy got a sunburn.

sweep

swallow

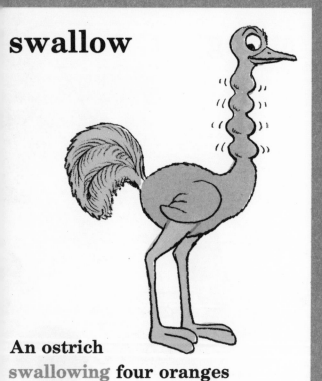

An ostrich
swallowing four oranges

swim

Fish do it.

sweaters

swing

T t

table
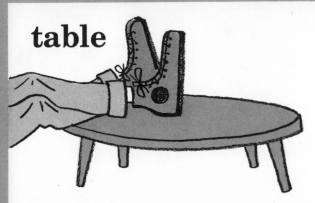
Feet on the table

tail

A long one

take

"Take those feet off that table."

talk

**Everybody talking
Nobody listening**

111

tall

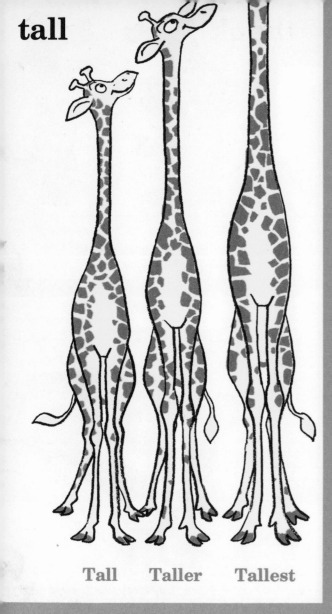

Tall   Taller   Tallest

taste

"This lemon tastes sour."

teach

Their teacher is teaching them to sing.

telephone

"Hello. Are you there?"

tame

Tame lion   Lion tamer

112

television

thank

"**Thanks**
for the thirteen tomatoes."

thermometer

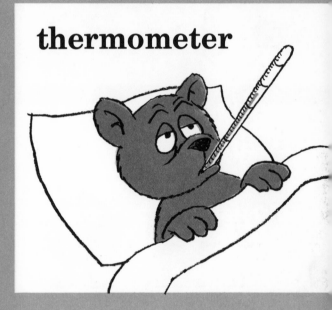

tell

"I will **tell** you again. I
told you before. NOT SO LOUD!"

thing

ten

Ten in a tent

113

think

A blue thing **thinking** about
a red thing

thread

throw

"Did you **throw** this?"

three

Three things

thumb

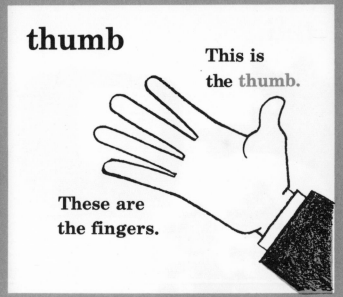

This is
the **thumb**.

These are
the fingers.

threw

He **threw** it
through the window.

tie

He **tied** the tiger tight.

time

"The time is now twelve to twelve."

tired

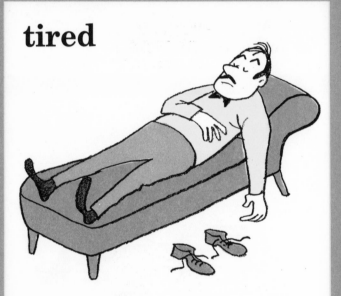

All tired out

today

Today is the twelfth.

Tomorrow is the thirteenth.

toe

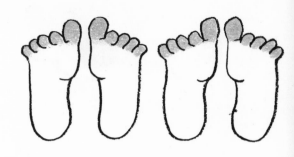

Twenty toes

tongue

too

Too fat

Too thin

115

tooth

Tooth

Teeth

Toothbrush

tower

A bear with a towel on top of a tower

top

"There is a green thing on top of my hat."

toy

Toy **town**

towel

A bear with a towel

train

Trains **run on tracks.**

tree

A red thing on a tree

truck

A truck full of rabbits

trick

My dog does tricks.

true

**Don't believe him.
It is not true.**

tricycle

trunk

An elephant's nose

try

"I will try to fly."

"I shouldn't have tried it."

turkey

Two turkeys talking

turn

Turning to the left

turtle

Turtles turning to the right

twins

typewriter

Typing a letter

U u

umbrella

Uncle Uriah is
under his umbrella.

up

He is up on a pole.
He is upside down.

us

"He makes us laugh."

underwear

Uncle Uriah is in
his underwear.

use

"We use him for a horse."

119

V v

vacation

"We are going on our vacation."

vacuum

Vacuum cleaner

vaccination

valentine

120

From Uncle Uriah to Aunt Ada

valley

Between two hills

village

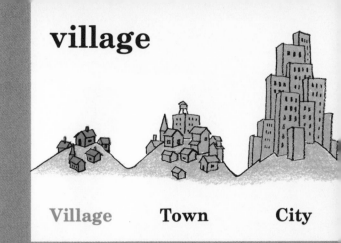

Village　　**Town**　　**City**

vanilla

Vanilla　　**Strawberry**

violin

very

A very, very, very small dog

volcano

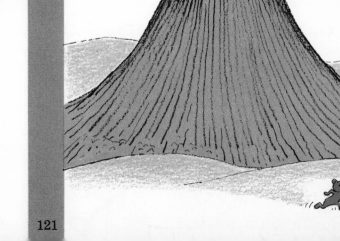

121

W w

wag

Wagging his tail

wait

"Wait! Wait! Wait for me!"

wagon

Wagging on a wagon

wake

She woke him up.

122

walk

Cats walking on a wall

walrus

A walrus
walking on a wall

warm

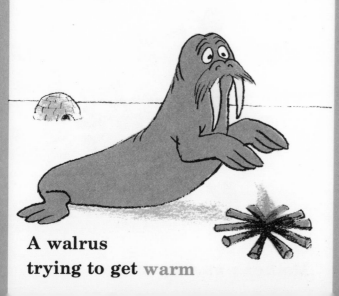

A walrus
trying to get warm

wash

Washing the baby

watch

Watching a watch

water

Aunt Ada likes the water.
She is riding on a wave.

way

"Get out of my way."

123

wear

We are wearing green hats.

went

We went out in the rain.

week

Seven days

wet

We came home wet.

weigh

How much do we weigh?

whack

Mother was very angry.

whale

The biggest animal there is

wheel

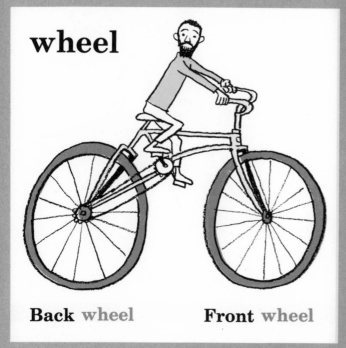

Back wheel   **Front** wheel

which

Which **twin is** which?

whisker

Cat's whiskers

whisper

A cat whispering

whistle

He comes when I whistle.

white

Black   White

why

WHY? WHY? WHY?
WHY? WHY?
WHY IS WATER WET?
WHY IS SNOW WHITE?
WHY DON'T COWS FLY?
WHY?
WHY?

He wants to know why.

win

Who will win, the turtle
or the rabbit?

wind

The wind came in the window.

wing

wink

wipe

"Wipe your feet."

wish

"I wish I had a hot dog."

won't

"I won't eat it."

with
without

With mustard   Without mustard

wood

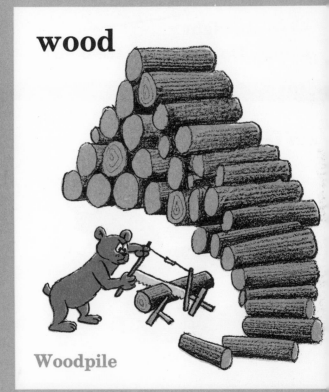

Woodpile

woman

One woman   Three women

wool

"My wool is woolly."

127

word

was
were
where
who
what
when
well
whose

Here are eight
words. Do you know them all?

would
wouldn't

I wouldn't like to be
a worm. Would you?

work

Hard work

write

I can write

world

Around the world

wrong

I KAN RITE

Aaron wrote it wrong.

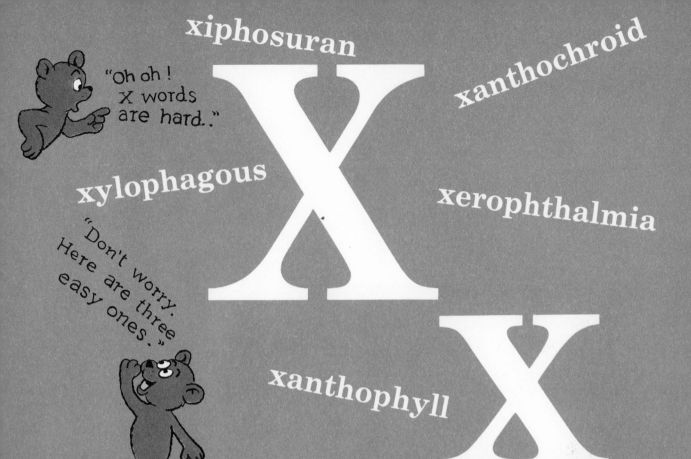

xiphosuran

xanthochroid

"Oh oh! X words are hard."

xylophagous

xerophthalmia

"Don't worry. Here are three easy ones."

xanthophyll

Xmas

A short word for Christmas

x-ray

X-ray looks inside you.

xylophone

129

Y y

yard

Three feet

yard

In our backyard
we have a hippopotamus.

yawn

Our hippopotamus
likes to yawn.

year

Twelve months

yes
yet

"Aren't you going to get up?"   "Yes, but not yet."

young

Young   Younger   Youngest

yell

I yell.   My dog yelps.

yellow

yoyo

Z z

zebras

zipper

"It's stuck.
I can't get out."

zero

zoo

Zero is very cold for zebras.

132

zyxuzpf

A nest full of zyxuzpf birds

five ax oar gargle Abigail crayon
igloo zoo
helicopter sandwich zipper camera
vanilla moon lollipops
xylophone splash lamb dentist
parachute listening
Mr. and Mrs. jack-o-lantern
xylophagous banana Eskimo elephant
rooster ear
queen lazy xanthochroid dry xerophthalmia
yawn yoyo Nubbglubb lamb too
wagon
honk package key volcano zoo
quack few pajamas
insect
dinosaur few grasshopper
zero groceries
alligator hungry Uriah
paw dad
rat quick camera giant
Minnihaweetonka underwear
saddle kerchoo ice cream use
overalls balloon mustard
cheese uncle dentist
eye zebras Aaron
glove mud kangaroo
dad jet freeze baby crayon